This book never fails . . .
Some people begin to yawn
before they get to letter B.
Others stay awake till P.
Nearly everyone is snoring
by the time they reach S.

**How many letters will there
be before you drop off?**

AWAKE

This is how you look now. It's natural: our book is just beginning.
Try closing your eyes for 3 seconds. Let's count . . . 1, 2, 3.
See? Nothing scary happened!

BRAIN

Sleep is a wonderful way to tidy up your brain.
Now it's buzzing with all the things you've done.
After just a few hours of sleep, everything will
be calm and in order again.

C

CAT

purrrrr

Can you curl up and purr like a little cat? Isn't it cosy?

DAY

Say goodbye to your day.
Talking and laughing,
running and walking,
playing and dancing:
let everything go.

Can you do it?

E
ENOUGH!

What do you say to someone who has been

running,

playing,

talking,

Woof! Woof!

singing,

joking and asking questions all day long?

F

FLY

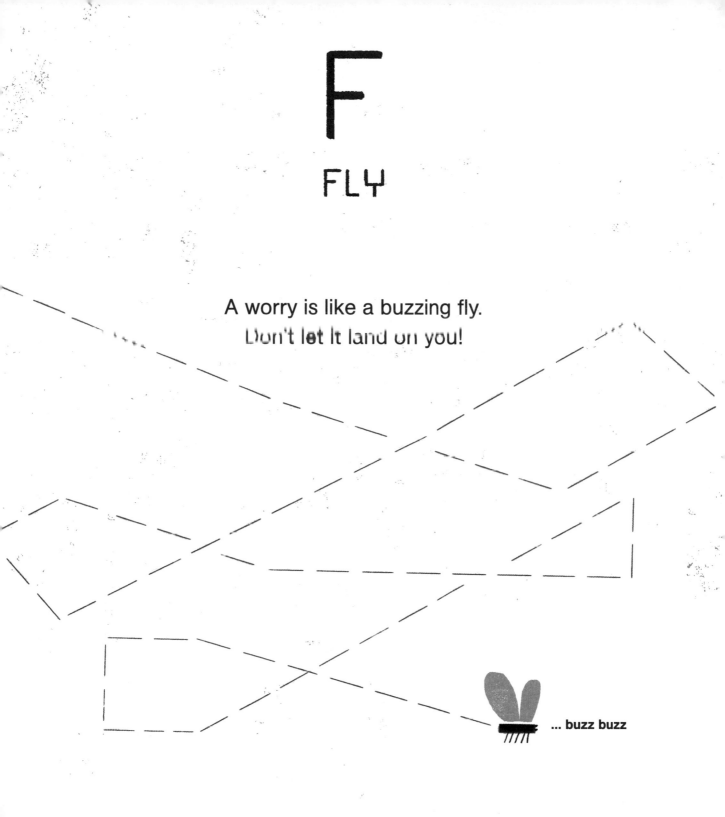

A worry is like a buzzing fly.
Don't let it land on you!

... buzz buzz

G

GOOD MORNING

When it's bedtime,
owls say gently
to their children:

good morning!

(but your parents aren't owls, are they?)

H

HIBERNATE

If you don't like sweet kittens, maybe you prefer fierce bears!

Did you know
that even the strongest bear
purrs to sleep when winter comes?

I

IMAGINE

Now we're somewhere warm and sunny . . .
Now your bed is a beautiful blue sea . . .
Now little waves are rocking you gently.

Let them rock you gently to sleep.

JUST ONE MORE

'Just one more in the bed?',
the little one said . . .

What do Mummy and Daddy think?

K
KISS

Everyone in the family needs a kiss before going to sleep.
Have you kissed everyone goodnight yet?
Is anyone still awake?

L
LEOPARD

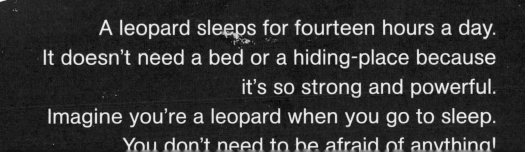

A leopard sleeps for fourteen hours a day.
It doesn't need a bed or a hiding-place because
it's so strong and powerful.
Imagine you're a leopard when you go to sleep.
You don't need to be afraid of anything!

MESSY

Some beds need a good rest by the time it's morning!

N

NEST

Have you seen this tiny blue bird before?

She's a little bird of sleep that comes at night to rest gently on the eyelids of very tired children.

What a special nest!

OFF-SWITCH

Not sleepy yet?
Do you still feel a tingle
in your toes?

Quick, find your off-switch!
Try pressing your nose.
Did that work?

click!

P

PEE

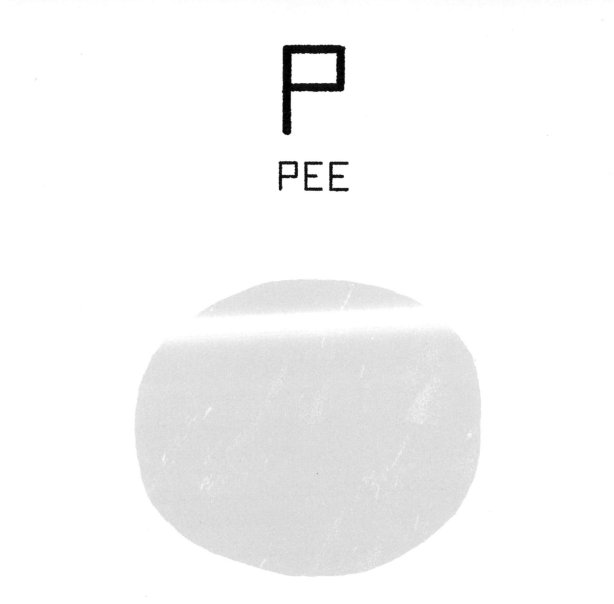

OK, this one is important. Did you go before you got into bed?

Q
QUIET

Think about what's quiet and it'll soon become quiet for you.
Imagine:
A cloud arrives on the other side of the window.
A cloud changes shape in the summer sky.

Closing your eyes is quiet too. Try it and see.

R

ROLL

Really wriggly kids roll around in bed.
Stay tucked in and sleep tight!

5
SNOOZE

Are you snoring yet, sleepyhead?
It's time to snuggle down and snooze.

T
TIME

When it's time to sleep here,
on the other side of the world it's time to wake up!
These children live thousands of miles away.

GOOD MORNING!

Are you still awake?
(While you don't go to sleep, morning won't arrive, you know.)

U

UPSIDE DOWN

It's fun playing upside down.
But now it's time to rest
so you can play again another day.

V

VACANT

Empty your attic,
sweep your rooms,
close the doors,
turn out the light.

Imagine
your head
completely
empty.

Nothing. No one. Never. None.

W

WISH

Wish upon
a star tonight.
Some children
sleep in the
shape of a star.

(And they twinkle,
of course
they do!)

Like they say:
'If you want to
stay bright, sleep
well this night!'

X

Oh no!

It took this boy so long
to think of a word beginning with X,
he fell asleep on the rug!

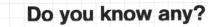 **Do you know any?**

Y
YAWN

Open your mouth as wide as you can.
Breathe in slowly.
And out again.
And again . . .

(Was that a yawn?)

ZZZz

That sound means that the book
has been switched off.

Everything around you is already asleep:
your shoes, your bag, your clothes, your books.

Turn yourself off too.
If you still haven't found your off-switch,
press this button here:

Well done!